BABY ANIMALS

BABY PENGUINS

Martha E. H. Rustad

Raintree is an imprint of Capstone Global Library Limited, a company incorporated in England and Wales having its registered office at 264 Banbury Road, Oxford, OX2 7DY – Registered company number: 6695582

www.raintree.co.uk
myorders@raintree.co.uk

Hardback edition © Capstone Global Library Limited 2022
Paperback edition © Capstone Global Library Limited 2023
The moral rights of the proprietor have been asserted.

All rights reserved. No part of this publication may be reproduced in any form or by any means (including photocopying or storing it in any medium by electronic means and whether or not transiently or incidentally to some other use of this publication) without the written permission of the copyright owner, except in accordance with the provisions of the Copyright, Designs and Patents Act 1988 or under the terms of a licence issued by the Copyright Licensing Agency, 5th Floor, Shackleton House, 4 Battle Bridge Lane, London SE1 2HX (www.cla.co.uk). Applications for the copyright owner's written permission should be addressed to the publisher.

Edited by Alison Deering
Designed by Jennifer Bergstrom
Original illustrations © Capstone Global Library Limited 2022
Picture research by Tracy Cummins
Production by Tori Abraham
Originated by Capstone Global Library Ltd

978 1 3982 2401 8 (hardback)
978 1 3982 2402 5 (paperback)

British Library Cataloguing in Publication Data
A full catalogue record for this book is available from the British Library.

Acknowledgements
We would like to thank the following for permission to reproduce photographs: Shutterstock: Bahadir Yeniceri, 21, bleung, 12, Eaks1979, 20 front, Enrique Aguirre, cover, Hay-woof, 19, jgolby, 15, Mario_Hoppmann, 6, Merrill McCauley, 13, photka, 20 back, robert mcgillivray, 7, Roger Clark ARPS, back cover, Samantha Crimmin, 5, takmat71, 9, Tetyana Dotsenko, 11, vladsilver, 16; SuperStock: Minden Pictures, 17.

Every effort has been made to contact copyright holders of material reproduced in this book. Any omissions will be rectified in subsequent printings if notice is given to the publisher.

All the internet addresses (URLs) given in this book were valid at the time of going to press. However, due to the dynamic nature of the internet, some addresses may have changed, or sites may have changed or ceased to exist since publication. While the author and publisher regret any inconvenience this may cause readers, no responsibility for any such changes can be accepted by either the author or the publisher.

WEST NORTHAMPTONSHIRE COUNCIL	
60000521468	
Askews & Holts	
BD	

Printed and bound in India

Contents

A new chick 4

Colonies 8

Feathers and fat 10

Swimming and hunting 14

All grown up 18

    Make a blubber glove 20

    Glossary 22

    Find out more 23

    Index 24

Words in **bold** are in the glossary.

A NEW CHICK

A male and female penguin keep an egg warm. They take turns sitting on it. Crack! The shell breaks. A baby penguin hatches out of the egg.

The fuzzy chick stays close to its parents. They take good care of it. They keep the baby warm in their cold **habitat**.

When the chick is hungry, it asks for food. Each chick has its own call. It taps on each parent's **bill** to ask for food.

The mother and father spit up food for their baby. Adult penguins only feed their own chicks.

COLONIES

Penguins live in groups. These are called **colonies**. Thousands of birds make nests in the same place. They come back to the same place each year.

Hungry parents leave their chicks to find food. Their chicks stay in a group called a **crèche**. Penguin chicks play together. They peck and fight. They huddle together if they get cold.

FEATHERS AND FAT

Penguin chicks have fuzzy feathers called **down**. Down can be white, grey, brown or black. Down should not get wet. Chicks must stay out of the water.

As they grow, chicks lose their fuzzy down feathers. At about 1 year old, new feathers grow in.

Penguins spread oil on their feathers using their bills. The oil comes from a body part near their tail. It makes their feathers waterproof.

Feathers help keep penguins warm. They trap air under their feathers to keep body heat in. **Blubber** also keeps penguins warm. Young penguins must eat a lot to build up this layer of fat.

SWIMMING AND HUNTING

Penguins do not fly. But they can swim very fast. They use their wings as flippers in the water.

Penguins swim and dive to catch fish and other **prey**. They dive underwater for as long as 20 minutes. Penguins must come up to breathe air.

Most penguins learn to swim on their own. Some chicks jump straight in. Others waddle in shallow water. Soon they will be able to swim and dive.

Young penguins also learn how to hunt. They eat fish, **krill**, shrimp and other animals. Some penguins hunt as a group. They push prey into a small area so it cannot get away.

ALL GROWN UP

Penguin chicks stay with their parents for a few weeks. Some stay for a year. Then it is time for the chick to go off on its own.

A penguin hunts, eats and grows. In a few years, it goes back to the place it hatched. Then it raises its own chicks. Penguins can live for up to 20 years.

MAKE A BLUBBER GLOVE

A layer of fat called blubber keeps penguins warm in cold water. Try making your own blubber glove to keep your hand warm.

What you need

- a bowl
- ice
- water
- two plastic freezer bags with a zip
- a spoon or spatula
- Lard or vegetable shortening

What you do

1. Fill a bowl with ice and water. Put your hand in the water. How does it feel?

2. Put a freezer bag on your hand. Use the spatula to spread a layer of lard or vegetable shortening on the bag. This layer of "fat" is like a penguin's blubber.

3. Place another freezer bag over the layer of lard or shortening.

4. Put your hand wearing the blubber glove into the bowl of cold water. How does it feel?

Glossary

bill hard front part of the mouth of a penguin

blubber thick layer of fat under the skin of penguins that keeps them warm

colony large group of animals that lives together in the same area

crèche group of young animals that gathers together

down soft, fluffy feathers of a penguin chick

habitat natural place and conditions in which an animal can live

krill small, shrimp-like animal

prey animal hunted by another animal for food

Find out more

Books

Penguins and Their Chicks (Animal Offspring), Margaret Hall (Raintree, 2018)

Penguins Are Awesome! (Polar Animals), Jaclyn Jaycox (Raintree, 2020)

Websites

www.bbc.co.uk/newsround/26688041
Find out more penguin facts with BBC Newsround.

www.dkfindout.com/uk/animals-and-nature/birds/penguins/
Learn more about penguins with DKFindout!

www.dkfindout.com/uk/animals-and-nature/birds/emperor-penguin/
Read about the largest penguin in the world, the emperor penguin.

Index

adulthood 18

bill 6, 12
blubber 13
breathing 14

colonies 8
crèche 8

diving 14, 16
down 10

eating 7–8, 13, 17, 18
egg 4

feathers 10, 12, 13
fish 14, 17
flippers 14

habitat 4
hatching 4, 18
hunting 8, 14, 17, 18

krill 17

lifespan 18

noises 6

playing 8
prey 14, 17

shrimp 17
swimming 14, 16

waterproof 12